Out of Darkness
Marc Little

for
my family.

without you these words
may never have been written

Acknowledgements

Some of these poems have appeared on www.fraido.wordpress.com and on www.writers-network.com.

My thanks to Mel McMahon, Mark Cassell, and Allen Farr and who unknowingly gave me the final push I needed to publish, and to Kay Heggarty, Leslie Millar, Jim Coffey, Pamela Reid, Gillian McClearn and Mark Radcliffe who always believed in me. I am a better person for having your friendship and support when I needed it the most.

Biography

Marc Little was born in Ballymena in 1973. Educated in Dunclug Primary School, Cambridge House Grammar School and the University of Ulster, in 1993 he joined the civil service rising to become the Chief Clerk for the County Court Divisions of Londonderry and Antrim in 2014. He is currently the Head of the Appeals Service in Northern Ireland.

He lives on the North Coast of Northern Ireland with his wife and family.

CONTENTS

Chapter 3 – Guard

Chapter 4 – Stability

Chapter 5 – Loss

Chapter 6 – Awakening

Epilogue

Prologue

Strangers

It's kind of funny that I cannot talk to others,
but I share my deepest thoughts with you.

It's kind of scary that so many of you read them,
and for some the feelings captured are not new.

I can't promise that I'll make it to tomorrow,
or even last the day, sad but true.

But if I do, I think I'll keep on sharing.
It might not help me,
but who knows it might help you.

Let you in

I'm fine as long as you don't ask.
Fine as long as you say nothing.

Don't question when I talk and when I stay silent,
and leave me in my own thoughts.

It's a difficult place for me to visit, my head.
Even more difficult to take you there.

So I'm fine as long as you don't ask,
and I'll let you visit, when I can.

A writer's accord

My words will always have meaning,
and be the truth in my head.
To not speak with honest conviction,
is to lie with my words that you've read.

I trust you to keep them in side you,
because that's where I found them,
in me.
Through time I pray I won't need them,
my own personal therapy.

Chapter 1 - Descent

Solitude

Gazing up through the branches,
The sky captured in random wooden frames.

Cold snow against my back,
finds a bare patch of skin on my neck.

Eyes close to create a memory,
and open with tears.

Recent memories and leaving here,
hurt.

Pills

Help me forget, can you do that?
Will you release me from my memories?
Will you release me?

Your size is deceptive.
Like an army, the more of you I use the greater the
chance of success.

A glass of water is the only reinforcement you need.

The moment

Know it.
Grasp it.
Feel it.
Cherish it.

When it ends,
let it go.

Then remember it,
and cry.

The truth

I lied when I said I was ok.
I lied when I said I was fine.
I lied when I said I'll get better.
I lied when I said I'd survive.

I lied when I said that I'd tell you,
when I'm ready to get some support.
I lie when I say that these words,
will be heard outside of my thoughts.

The end

A life that has lost any purpose,
my will to keep living is gone.
The desire to bring a conclusion,
to this pathetic existence is strong.

After thousands of years of evolution
work, sleep, work, sleep, little more.
What's the point of it really I ask you,
what the hell is it all for?

When I think of my place on this planet,
it barely resembles a tick.
I think I'll simply erase it,
and be sure that I end it real quick!

Sanity

Sleepless nights,
restless days.
Constant thinking
life replayed.

Alternative routes,
said no and not yes?
Been content, never happy,
my being supressed?

Frustrated inaction,
or living life full?
Routine never ending,
or together the fool?

Are things that much better?
Has my life changed that much?
What's important, my sanity,
or the things I gave up?

What keeps me here?

I look over the edge, close my eyes and see your future.

I have only just left.
Tears on your face, uncontrollable sobbing.
The question "why?" repeated over and over, never
answered.
You are inconsolable, the loss unbearable.

You're older now, reading my name on stone.
He holds your hand as you tell him about me.
Aging memories release emotions,
causing smiles and tears between your words.
He squeezes your hand and promises never to leave
you,
like your father did.

You're older still.
Fading memories of me form stories you tell your
children.
Your thoughts create tinges of sadness, even now.
"So much missed dad."
Hurt still surface when you are alone, tears still flow.
"Why?" never answered.

I open my eyes and step back from the edge.

You are asleep when I return,
curled up in your bed surrounded by animals.
I lightly kiss your forehead,

a tear lands on your cheek.
My question answered.

Escape

I'm running,
can you see me?
That's me heading north!
To a place no one will find me,
no person, fear, or thought.

No burdens on my shoulders,
or sinking feelings around my waist.
No despair or quiet weeping,
they can't keep up as I make haste!

I'll use this stream ahead of me,
to wash them off my scent.
Then disappear to silence,
as I make my final sprint.

I'm sleeping now,
tread softly,
respect this home of mine.
Lay flowers but be happy,
I've left the hell behind.

Talk myself down

I'm not about to jump,
well I'm scared of heights.
Can't overdose on drugs,
I've lost my appetite.
There's no hangman's drop,
in case my head comes off.
Won't be slitting my wrists,
much too messy a job.

Hypothermia's good,
but you end up blue.
Electrocutions quick,
but puts the bills up too.
Drownings hard to arrange,
30 miles from the sea.
As for shooting one's self,
way too violent for me.

I'd jump in front of a train,
but the rush hour's hell.
Hire a hitman to do me,
might kill the neighbour as well.

I never knew this part,
would be a pain in the ass.
Think I'll live some more,
until the feelings pass.

Courage

I dare to be happy.
I date to be free.
I dare to cry "no more!"
I dare to be,
me.

Youth

That face can't be mine?
It's old and torn,
that's not me?
But there's an impish mind,
behind that old smile,
it's still young,
and fresh,
and free!

Money tree,
messy room,
forest forts,
and sweets.
Spaceship travels,
ray gun battles,
"be home in time,
for tea!"

Tree top standing,
wheelie crash landing.
Rope swings,
at river banks.
Skateboard sailing,
robber jailing.
Water fights,
and pranks!

That face maybe mine,

though aged & lined,
its me.
Holstered ray guns,
poised to fight.
Still young,
still fresh,
still free.

Chapter 2 - Rising

Writers block

My thoughts are bare and silent,
Inspiration's gone astray.
The gift of writing down some words,
has up and gone away.

Where once the words came easy,
Now they struggle to be free.
It seems my dark emotions,
Released them easily.

Maybe I should be grateful,
for this symptom I display?
To have respite from the darkness,
may help me see another day.

A poem

I wrote you a poem,
in the hope that you might read,
all the words I dare not say,
on the occasions,
that we meet.

I wrote you a poem,
exposing my heart and soul.
Your beauty mutes my voice stone dead,
complete me,
make me whole.

I wrote you a poem,
a collection of letters, words & verse,
together they have one meaning,
you are,
my universe.

I wrote you a poem,
I'll wrap it up real quick.
A four letter word beginning with "L?"
I'll close my eyes,
and let you pick.

Which way is up?

Oh crap.
I can't get my head straight.
I don't know if I'm crazy,
or sick.
The routine of life,
just means nothing.
Someone please give my ass,
a huge kick.

If that doesn't work,
then a doctor.
He might give me some tablets,
instead.
I'm told that they lessen the madness,
and the voices that talk,
in my head.

Let's be clear,
when I use the word
"voices,"
as a matter of fact,
it's just mine.
I can't shut up and stop thinking!
A symptom of,
losing my mind?

I know the cause,
of this illness,
but the cure is a price,

I won't pay.
There are others like me,
on this planet.
Love affects us all,
the same way.

I guess,
I'll just suffer in silence.
and hope my brain,
won't erupt.
Right now,
I'm all muddled and love struck.
Please help me.

Which way is up?

Inside my head

If I let you in my head,
would you promise not to tell,
any of the secrets,
that you find?

Would you keep it to yourself,
that I'm not the happy elf,
who laughs and jokes,
with others in real life?

Can you find it in your heart,
of my sadness to depart,
from convention,
don't tell it to the world.

And when you finally get your teeth,
and you see what lies beneath,
don't run away or hide,
stay a while.

Timing

If you think about things too much,
you can lose the moment.
If you look at all the options before deciding,
you can miss your chance.
If you give up the fight before the last ring of the bell,
you can lose the girl.

Together

Wherever you are you can still see the stars,
and feel a light breeze on your face.

Wherever you are you can still catch the moon,
and the touch of a hand soft as lace.

Wherever you are shooting stars will appear,
and light up a dark winters night.

Wherever you are I'll be there at your side,
night after night after night.

Walk with me

Walk with me.
You're part of my soul.
You here at my side,
makes me calm,
makes me whole.
Helps me face what's ahead,
with the strength to defend.
all that you are,
with my very last breath.

Walk with me,
And all that I am,
will like naked and open,
like the palm of my hand.
That I'll ask you to take,
and hold to your heart,
So I can feel every beat,
and touch every part.

Walk with me,
and we'll travel together,
through good times and strife.
for I long to be with you,
for the rest of my life.

The little things

Tell me that you love me,
Touch my arm or stroke my neck.
Hold my hand when we are walking,
give my cheek a little peck.

Smile when we're together,
and melt my aching heart.

Please tell me that you love me,
before I fall apart.

Me

Take me as I am.
I'm all I have to give.
A person who's just skin and bone,
There's nothing more than me.
I make mistakes,
and get things wrong.
Talk when silence is needed.
Get insecure,
say the wrong things.
Sorry gets repeated.

My flaws are bare and open,
I'm exactly what you see.
I've no backdoors,
no hidden sides.

I'm sorry.

I'm just me.

Hold me

The world contains wonders,
breath taking to see.
But nothings more stunning,
than your arms around me.

Asleep

I feel you softly breathing,
your skin against my skin.
In the silence of the darkness,
the depth of my feelings sinking in.

A smile grows slowly on my face,
as my mind begins to dream.
It takes me from the room we're in,
to places where we've been.

To star lit skies where shooting stars,
caused gasps and laughs of delight.
To rolling seas we watched on rocks,
and marvelled at the sight.
To forest paths and fallen leaves,
we walked among at dusk.
To a clear blue lake where on a boat,
we fought the wind,
and lost!

The morning sounds awake me,
my night wanderings subside.
More memories to be created,
as more and more I feel alive!

Soulmate

A mythical beastie,
whose gender don't matter.
May be tall, short or skinny.
They're highly sought after.

They'll listen adeptly,
to all of your woes.
Won't judge, criticise you,
they'll go with the flow.

Understanding and patience,
skills they'll use every day.
Your faults?
"Who you are!"
they'll reassuringly say.

Pull you close when you need it,
and laugh when you don't.
They're truthful and honest,
dependable folk.

Set your traps and go hunting,
they're numbers are few.
If your caught, don't struggle,
it just might be you.

Chapter 3 - Guard

Relapse

It never really goes.
It hides,
plotting escape,
awaiting weakness.
When found,
it's return is overwhelming.

Feeding on despair,
it grows stronger.
Reserves of optimism,
overcome in the first wave.
Thoughts of others,
all that prevails.

It retreats to its lair,
new plans to make.
I fear one day,
it will win,
and by my demise
cause its own.

Why?

Why do some thoughts revolve in my head?
Why at times do they fill me with dread?
Why do they fear what my future holds?
Why do they sometimes refuse to let go?

Why do others seem to get all the breaks?
Why do I feel there's no more I can take?

Why am I not alone in my thoughts?
Why am I here when others are not?
Why am I me and why all these questions?
Why isn't "easy" in life's equation?

The descent

There are,

too many things,
running through my head.
Too many things,
trying to be said.
Too many things,
working themselves out.
Too many things,
filling me with doubt.

Too many things,
crowding rational thought.
Too many things,
needing to be fought.
Too many things,
making my mood low.
Too many things,
pushing me to go.
Too many things,
a room, of ticking clocks.
Too many things,
I need them all,
to stop!

Too many things,
drowning out what's me.
Too many things,
a mad cacophony.

Too many things,
my soul cries out,
"No more!"
Too many things,
silenced by the roar.

Too many things,
these words may never end.
Too many things,
I write my own portend.

Pebbles

A few words,
written on stone.
Painful memories to be erased.

Names, places, thoughts,
consigned to small letters,
Expunged from the mind.

From the shore,
the pebbles fly,
returning to the sea.

Sinking into the abyss,
the ocean envelopes,
the past.

Chapter 4 - Stability

My day

I'll wake at nine on normal days,
and wash under rainbows!
Then sit and stare at blue giraffes,
until the doorbell goes.

The singing penguins have arrived,
Groucho, Karl and Mo.
To serenade with songs of love,
and Beatles songs they know.

When they're done, by half past two,
they waddle off for lunch.
In their place two apes appear,
with bananas by the bunch!

Delights of milkshake heaven,
they rustle up by four.
Just in time for Attila the Hun
to bang upon my door!

Not a one for primates,
he'll shoo the guys away.
He'll wash up all the mess they made,
and engage me on my day.

We talk until the little hand,
hovers close to nine.
"To bed" he'll growl with heavy heart,
for me it's supper time!

The house is calm and peaceful,
once fed to bed I go.
I smile about the life I live,

when my medications low.

Arrival

Time to get wipes and some nappies.
Booties, bottles and bibs.
Babygro's, rattles and blankets.
Soft fluffy toys,
and a crib.

High chair, car seat and clothing.
Buggy with waterproof top.
Steriliser, formula, rusks.
Changing mat,
cream for your bot.

A huge bunch of flowers for mum,
who's body's exhausted and sick.
A bucket of love when you get here,
and one wish,
make 9 months come quick!

The date

My clothes are all ironed,
I'm showered and shaved.
Got a head so excited,
I nearly missed my train.
For this afternoon,
our news is delivered.
The date that you'll get here,
my lip starts to quiver.

It's the day we're awaiting,
the time's almost done,
when I can look at my love,
and say,
"this is our son."

A penny a page

A penny a page.
Each page a new memory,
recorded forever,
by developing hands.
Small slivers of fingers,
catch time as it passes.
Experiences, feelings,
all stored in your mind.

A penny a page.
We'll add to your story.
Our characters playing,
the role of two guides.
With another to help us,
we'll write down some chapters.
A sizeable piece,
in the book of your life.

A penny a page.
Let's make your book priceless.
With infinite stories,
and words that abound!
A book of adventure,
of love and excitement.
A book of the life,
that we'll build for our child.

I could

I could write about clouds,
white as snow drops,
and say they're as soft as your skin.
Then include how the beauty of nature,
is overpowered by your smile,
or a grin.

Perhaps include lines from
Will Shakespeare,
for "heaven is here,
where you live."
Or words from own composition,
"all I have, all I am,
I will give."

My words could fill up the heavens,
and still they'd be,
way too few!
So for now I'll settle with,
Boo!

Guess what?

It's me!

I love you.

Stars

Random lights in the black canopy.
The emotions of a world,
spilled under their gaze.

Words said by thousands,
replayed and repeated forever.

Their beauty,
calming.

Natures therapy for imperfect souls.

The sea

Powerful beauty,
breath-taking when calm,
humbling when stirred.

The guardian

Immovable patience,
watching waves & tides.
Gentle breeze,
raging seas,
sculpts his face,
through time.

Bodies wrapped,
then bare skin,
clamber on rock,
as summer begins.
Unsteady feet
starting to slip,
fingers deftly,
searching for grip.

Gulls glide,
in blue skies,
perch on top,
as the sun dies.
The Guardian presides,
over all,
it surveys.
A perpetual sentinel,
along,
the causeway.

Reality

The truth is,
no one gives a shit.
The truth is,
no one cares.
The truth is,
they'll only give a damn,

if you wear your underwear.....

Upon your head,
wrapped around each arm,
in fact anywhere that's not,
at the top of your legs around your waist.
covering your bot!

For them you're an annoyance,
an embarrassment, a pain.
Your foolishness too much on show,
your mad you've gone insane!

Keep your underwear where it should be,
your feelings not on show.
They all have lives they need to live,
no one really wants to know.

The feign of being interested,
of always "being there!"
In truth depends on one small thing.
Where you wear your underwear!

Dreams

Tell me your dreams,
are they scary or nice?
Do they make you laugh loudly,
or cry in the night?

Are they all to be shared?
Maybe some you should hide,
for fear of revealing,
what goes on in your mind.

If you note them all down,
would they struggle and fight,
to appear on the pages,
in the words you might write?

Perhaps they'd flow freely
and fill up a book.
You might read when you're older,
on the path your life took.

Tell me your dreams,
and I'll tell you mine,
a myriad of emotions,
from the mad to benign.

A range that's quite scary,
yet one theme overrides'
amidst all the mayhem,
our futures combined.

Butterflies

When you do things that might make me angry,
with the intention of making things right.
Surprise me with sparks of excitement,
or reach out and squeeze my hand tight.

Head on the pillow, eyes closed, sleeping.
In the midst of some trees in the wood.
Staring at waves in the ocean,
with the rain dripping down from your hood.

Butterflies surge with emotion,
and overcome me whenever you're near.
Lean your head gently down on my shoulder,
let me whisper three words in your ear.

Child

Raise your head,
I can't see.
Cowering conceals
feelings etched in expression,
framing your ordeal.

Speak up,
I can't hear.
Mumbling hides,
reasons to be given,
for the tears in your eyes.
Calm down,
I can't know.
Pandemonium belies,
distillation of words,
where the truth resides.

Come closer,
I can't hug.
Distance prevents,
comfort in oneness,
a shoulder for laments.

Chapter 5 - Loss

In memoriam

He was born to loving parents,
had siblings, loved them dear.
He went to school until he left,
then had a job for years.

He fell in love, had children,
shared happy times, and tears.
They grew up quick, he never felt,
the passing of the years.

Before too long the grand kids came,
he loved them like his own.
But time was catching up with him,
arthritis in his bones.

With treatment he kept going,
but age you can't escape.
The reaper took him in the night,
he died at 68.

If this story seems familiar,
it's because it's kind of true.
Project yourself some years ahead,
it could be me or you!

Grandmother
Dedicated to Theresa Fusco

The rock the storms of life,
couldn't tarnish.
The rock that remained,
steadfast and true.
That rock that anchored a family,
together.
The rock that protected,
while life around grew.

The rock that repelled,
the harsh words of others.
The rock that gave comfort,
with laughter and tea!
The rock that time ravaged,
but whose light shone relentless!
The rock the foundation,
from which we all grew.

My friend
Dedicated to Jim Smith

I'll never forget, your soft words of comfort.
I'll never forget, the peace you'd imbue.
I'll never forget, your jokes, lame & puny.
I'll never forget, your laugh, deep & true.

I'll never forget, looking up when we're talking.
I'll never forget, being small beside you.
I'll never forget, your child like demeanour.
I'll never forget, your mischievousness too!

I'll never forget, your heart, always giving.
I'll never forget, your face, etched to care.
I'll never forget, your friendship, un-wanting.
I'll never forget, say your name, you were there.

I'll never forget, the nights doubled over.
I'll never forget, the pain in our sides.
I'll never forget, the tears of pure laughter.
I'll never forget the friend by my side.

I'll never forget,
because they all grow inside me,
and in all of the hearts,
that your soul lightly kissed.
I'll never forget,
until I breath my last breath,
never forgotten,
perpetually missed.

Hero
Dedicated to Lawrence Cadden

Your epitaph taught me so much,
a life touched yet completely unknown.
Words from family describing,
a benevolent, altruistic, pure soul.
A life evolved around hardship,
physical, emotional, and more.
Not bitter, or resentful, only caring,
dedication to others, life's goal.

You're smiles didn't hide pain or suffering,
they reflected real joy from within.
Genuine, ignited from a passion,
to see all the good life can bring.
Tears from all who bore witness,
to words overflowing with grace.
Our honour to have called friend, a hero,
immortal in inspired words, acts, and deeds.

The funeral

Moist eyes and silent words.
Returning images from those who remember,
respectful ignorance and curiosity from those who
cannot.
The gathering of the living.

A lifetime of embraces,
imprinted on the host.
Embalmed in white silk, oak, and brass.
Eyes focused where they rest.
The repository of the past.

Ethereal essence, adrift.
Touching, growing, teaching.
Gone, yet remaining, passed,
yet returning.
The living deceased.

Clichés to the broken

Clichés to the broken,
silent words spoken.
Time in slow motion,
tears for lives stolen.

Clichés for the broken,
compassion awoken.
Raging grief potent,
relentless emotion.

Clichés for the broken,
lost in an ocean.
The future unwoven,
a life spent coping.

Clichés for the broken,
memories beholden.
A new path chosen.
The next chapter opens.

Chapter 6 - Awakening

Sabbatical

I haven't written in a while,
no reason,
I suppose.
Forcing letters to combine,
ain't a way to write,
good prose.

Words should flow,
like fizzy pop,
spilling from a glass.
Sporadic wit and humour,
popping out,
like gas!
Fall into place,
chaos in grace,
like a 9am,
Monday morning,
commuter.

How letters gather,
to tell a tale,
follows no reason
or rhyme.
Be patient and wait,
let the words
congregate.
Genius may come,

if it's time!

Simple things

Simple ideas.
Simple times.
Simple words.
Simple rhymes.
Simple fears.
Simple minds.
Simple stories.
Simple lines.

Simple pathways.
Simple boots.
Simple choices.
Simple routes.
Simple thinking.
Simple knots.
Simple hopes.
Simple thoughts.

Simple nights.
Simple days.
Simple living.
Simple ways.
Simple future.
Simple past.
Simple present.
Simple task?

Simply wants.
Simply meanings.

Simply needs.
Simply feelings.
Simply dreaming.
Simply free.
Simply hopeful.
Simply, me.

They say

That's what they say.
It's the way it's done.
There's no point in arguing.
The race is almost run.
It's taking part that matters.
There are no losers here.
Listen to your elders.
Pin back those ears.

If I could I'd do it for you.
A stitch in time saves nine.
Hold your horses buddy.
There's no such thing as mine.
Share and share alike.
A nice word spreads a smile.
The party's just beginning.
Me, I'd run a mile!

Nothing in life is free,
and the early bird catches the worm.
Don't come running to me.
Hold your ground, stand firm!
Keep your head held high.
Pride comes before a fall.
If you can't say anything pleasant,
then just say nothing at all!

The void

I'm searching for my other,
they who by my side,
walked amongst,
the multitude,
downbeat,
but head held high.

Wrapped around,
a weakened soul,
that naked to the world,
would wither and disintegrate,
without my others hold.

Their courage,
unimpeachable,
compelled to keep it safe.
Protective unrelenting care,
despite my others,
fate.

Cast aside,
when needs abate,
as pretenders to our struggle,
cushion, comfort, half the soul,
narcissistic,
to our humble.

Where once at night,
we sang our tunes,

to steel us for the dawn.
I lie alone my tears sing silent,
sonnets,
for life's pawn.

I'm alone now,
odd,
this feeling is.
Where always two now one.
A refuge in an ocean world,
half my world,
undone.

I await the reaper,
to seal my fate,
vacant and unemployed.

For what use is one unmatched sock,
when my others lost,
into,
the void?

The river

There's a river runs,
from start to end,
on either side we play.
With ball and bat,
and pen and thought,
it changes day by day.
Alone in travel,
or hand in hand,
we cross the flowing time.
Stand, walk, run, fall,
a melodic,
lifetime rhyme.

Connections made,
heart to heart,
friend, or sometimes foe.
Collect with events,
experiences, laments,
as we move,
shore to meadow.
A future unknown,
unfolds as we go,
consequences,
a few unintended.
Some bridges used,
shouldn't all be burned,
when found,
some,
need to be mended.

Discarded lands,
or forgotten souls,
the past inherits today,
Moulding, changing,
all that we are,
our emotional id DNA.
The length of our journey,
counted in breaths,
the last gasp,
maybe moments away.
So cross between shores,
and sail ever north,
the sea of dreams,
can be reached,
in a day.

The Rock star

Sings aloud the world to hear,
lungs bursting to capacity.
Verses, bridge, chorus in sync,
but question the veracity,
of the song in tune,
though the rhyme imbues,
to lead a heavy rock band.
Head movements in time,
facial gestures a crime,
obscene, yet Rock star divine.

Hands beat a rhythm,
feet tap together,
scarily far from the pedals.
Inside the domain,
of the in-car sensation.

The Legend.

The Rock star.

The Rebel!

Sleepy time

Time to get some sleepy time,
close my eyes and dream.
Wake refreshed, revitalised,
that's the hope it seems?
Truth is when the alarm goes off,
I'll be more tired and cranky,
I may resort to softcore violence,
and give my phone a hard spanky,
with a baseball bat, some gasoline and a match,
saved, just for the occasion.
When it comes to the union of night time and day,
I'll always vote for secession.

To stay under-cover, while the world muddles on,
and sleep until sometimes midday.
That's what I need until I find that I'm able,
to join in life's joyful foray!

So close your eyes and have sweet dreams,
keep the bogey man at bay.
If the bedbugs bite, burn their ass,
and send them on their way.
You may not wake alert with a smile,
that shit was never true.
Tired and cranky has it's plus side,
when the world needs to hear a
"screw you!"

Grrrrrrr

The extras

We are all burgeoning actors.
We are all stars on the cusp.
We are all destined for greatness.
We are all statuesque hunks.
We are all made for the movies.
We are all going to go far.
We are all about to be famous.
We are all soon to be superstars.

We are all squeezed in together.
We are all non-descript.
We are all lined up like cattle.
We are all herded and shipped.
We are all searching for glory.
We are all imagining lights around our name.
We are all stepping onto the ladder.
We are all seeking fortune and fame.

For now we all sit and share stories.
For now we all try and stay warm.
For now we all make fun of divas.
For now we all watch professionals perform.
For now we all live in the real world.
For now we all had, just a whiff.
For now we all top up our coffees.
For now we all dream of what if?

Cheers!

I've had a drink.
Ok more than one.
But way less than ten (so far!),
my head yearns for fun.
Random giggles escape,
at the daftest of things.
Concentration, forget it!
I've a soul set to sing!
These legs want to boogie,
though standings problematic.
Music choice doesn't matter,
I'm a whomever fanatic (their biggest fan!).
Overemphasised speaking,
every word said sssp....sssp...specific.
Intensive eye contact,
my talking's prolific.
The world's getting smaller,
peripheral vision shot to hell.
Outlook? Hell it's rosy!
In the cosmos I dwell.
The bottles near finished,
mixers all done.
Off licence closed early,
at the a.m. of one.
Pit stop, I'm unconscious.
Sedations set in.
This tale finished later.
Sheesh...the mess I am in.

It takes time

There's a sailor on the ocean,
head bent towards the sky,
gazing at the heavens,
stars reflected in his eyes.
Light from the past, has travelled,
for eons just to be,
in that time, in that moment,
for the sailors eyes to see.

In the desert wind uncovers,
footprints cast in stone,
found by a team of scholars,
from a past Jurassic zone.
Walked, imprinted, waiting,
for millions of years it seems,
for that time, for that moment,
for all mankind to see.

Across a room glances converge,
strangers for many years,
soon embark on life combined,
share laughter, love and tears.
Their journeys crossed, at a junction,
paths combined emotionally,
for a time, for a moment,
for each other's hearts to see.

Chaos reigns around our heads,
space and time collide.

Random chance or designer led,
the universe sublimes.
Moments framed in emotion,
beauty framed in time.
Stop, rest, touch your life,
in feelings, thoughts and rhyme.

Humanity lost

Sardines inside the can,
bad smells from one or two.
Stay upright with good fortune,
manners only from a few.
Hawk eyes seek salvation,
each stop with speed they fly.
An empty seat a diamond,
win their prize or die!

Loud voices talk to others,
at some place far from here.
Privacy forgotten,
way too much said, I fear.
The deaf play music loudly,
from which there's no escape.
While old folk breathe the fetid air,
gasping, mouths agape.

The jailer surveys the captives,
their dignity defiled.
"Tickets please" he orders,
as we continue our train ride.

Golden

Dominoes & tartan rugs.
Flasks of tea & warm oversized mugs.
Bingo in the Common Room.
Gardening lessons start at noon.
Rails installed to prevent falls.
Nurse & vicar do their calls.
Photographs of three generations,
sharing space with medication.
Orthopaedic chair facing telly,
hand written note making sense of the many,
channels to choose in this digital world,
sound turned up loud to ensure that it's heard!
Porcelain ornaments placed on shelf spaces,
immune from high temperatures causing red faces,
on visitors to the home of the couple,
cosy and warm,
in their elderly bubble!

Ups and downs

Select your floor,
squeezing past all the others.
Bodily odours begin to smother,
your lungs as they gasp,
for fresh air to breathe.
"Get out of my space!"
you inwardly plea.
Nudges, pushes,
testing your patience.
Oh for a place a little more spacious.
Do they only make elevators in "tiny?"
For the claustrophobic masochistic, mad folk.
Blimey!

Royalty would never choose,
this form of travel.
All squashed in together,
the posh with the rabble.
No etiquette, social norm,
rule books to follow.
Get in, choose a floor,
a macrocosmic fiasco.
Is that a real person,
who recites words that proper,
as she counts out the floors,
like a Queen to us paupers.

"Just take the stairs, and don't be so whiny!"
That's what you're thinking,

and not to unwisely.
I would,
but in this fast food world that's called lazy,
by floor two I'd be gasping,
my eyesight all hazy.
If I made it to five, by giving my best,
the most I could hope for,
cardiac arrest!

So I'll slum with my fellow,
unhealthy companions,
as I vertically travel,
with reckless abandon,
and I'll try not to punch the chap from floor seven,
who's rucksack swung around & wiped out my mate
Kevin.
Left a wife, a dog,
two cats, a gerbil,
and two teeth on the carpet,
a horrible purple.
I'll pray for the day,
I can work down below,
and travel to work in,
a small bungalow!

Make it real

Imagine a moment.
Hold it in your hands.
Close your eyes and dream that it's real,
then make it so.

Epilogue

Journey

Where the birds fly.
Where the rivers flow.
Where the sun sets.
Where the time goes.

Where the day breaks.
Where the night falls.
Where the moon rises.
Where the wolf calls.

When my heart races.
When my stomach churns.
When my knees go weak.
When I go so red it burns.

When my sleep is restless.
When my thoughts won't stop.
When my concentrations gone.
When I sing a lot!

Where shooting stars land.
Where the lightning strikes.
Where there's no race to run.
Where there's no need to fight.

Where our dreams go.
Where our journey begins.
Where the future starts.

Where everyone wins.

My whole being is peaceful,
as your holding my hand.
Taking small steps together,
our destination is planned.
Over green fields and valleys,
over blue seas we'll go.
In my mind I finally see us.
living over the rainbow.

Mel McMahon was born in Lurgan in 1968. His work appeared widely in journals and anthologies and has been broadcast on BBC Radio Ulster.

He has been short-listed for several literary prizes and was a prize-winner in the FSNI Poetry Competition (2015).

His work has been nominated twice for the Forward Prize for best individual poem. His first collection, *Out of Breath*, was published by Summer Palace Press in 2016. His second collection, *Beneath our Feet*, poems written in commemoration of Wilfred Owen was published in 2018.

He is currently Head of English at the Abbey Grammar School, Newry, County Court.

Mark Cassell lives in a rural part of the UK where he often dreams of dystopian futures, peculiar creatures, and flitting shadows. Primarily a horror writer, his steampunk, dark fantasy, and SF stories have featured in several anthologies and ezines.

His best-selling debut novel, *The Shadow Fabric*, is closely followed by the popular short story collection, *Sinister Stitches*, and are both only a fraction of an expanding mythos of demons, devices, and deceit.

The dystopian sci-fi short story collection, *Chaos Halo 1.0: Alpha Beta Gamma Kill*, is in association with Future Chronicles Photography where he works closely with their models and cosplayers.

His work has been compared with British horror authors such as James Herbert, Clive Barker, Dennis Wheatley, and Brian Lumley. Also, his influences spread over to the US where he admits to having been first inspired by Dean Koontz, Stephen King, Dan Simmons, and H P Lovecraft.

www.markcassell.co.uk

Made in the USA
Middletown, DE
29 November 2022

16333248R00055